# Beyond the Lords
# &
# The New Creatures

# Beyond the Lords

# &

# The New Creatures

Forrest Parker

Writer's Showcase
San Jose  New York  Lincoln  Shanghai

## Beyond the Lords & The New Creatures

Writer's Showcase
an imprint of iUniverse.com, Inc.

For information address:
iUniverse.com, Inc.
5220 S 16th, Ste. 200
Lincoln, NE 68512
www.iuniverse.com

ISBN: 0-595-15749-1

Printed in the United States of America

# "The Mind Opened Will Never Close"

## Introduction:

This is the door that I have opened. This is what came to me once I peered in. Others will view it differently but to me, they have only opened their own mental doorways and saw what came to them individually. This is my sense in direction as it relays to me now, it could change, I don't know. The only thing I'm sure of is that I'm not sure…To me Jim Morrison's writings were a conscious effort to begin a piece of written work that would have no known end, they where thought provoking bodies of incomplete literature, intended to stimulate each receiving persona to open their own mental perceptions to view their own translations and states of mind within cognitive processes both conscious and subconsciously. Opening one doorway only leads to another in the pathway of existence and mental awareness. My vision of these processed thoughts, generated originally by Mr. Morrison's beginning words, is only continued by me in what he started, it is not in anyway, finished but only @ what I found to be the second door of awareness for myself. I ask that all of you reading take the core of what he wrote and dissect it for yourself in your own direction & processes. Read what I have added and if you follow, continue on by opening your own doorways to the next levels attainable in thought, realization & perceptions. If your own collectiveness takes you another direction @ any time, be receptive to yourself and follow it to where it leads.
Nothing truly ever ends…
A Journey is a Journey of Journeys.
Awareness is only the beginning of a realized new depth.
Sincerely,

Forrest Parker

**Mr. Morrison's original writings are designated in Arial Bold Font.**

Mr. Parker's interpreted additions generally follow as such.

"Thought makes everything fit for use."

Ralph Waldo Emerson

**Look where we worship.**

See before you praise.
Dance before you commit.
Give not to give but to be.
Fall into that which has always been to find you.
Now a part of all, rejoice amongst the Universal Heaven.

**We all live in the city.**

**The city forms-often physically, but inevitably psychically-a circle. A Game. A ring of death with sex at its center. Drive toward outskirts of city suburbs. At the edge discover zones of sophisticated vice and boredom, child prostitution. But in the grimy ring immediately surrounding the daylight business district exists the only real crowd life of our mound, the only street life, nightlife. Diseased specimens in dollar hotels, low boarding houses, bars, pawn shops, burlesques and brothels, in dying arcades which never die, the streets and streets of all night cinemas.**

The same show plays again and again. Changing in character but not in plot, chaos has always spawned life through disorder, born from the loins of that which has never been correct.

**When play dies it becomes the Game.**
**When sex dies it becomes Climax.**

From sleep follows the Awakening.
In vision comes the Focus.
In fear comes only the Fright.

When it's over, it is not.

Pass through nothingness open only to the light of being.

Retain all that is true in heart as conclusions birth only a new direction, in any ending, is only found yet another way.

**All games contain the idea of death.**

Winner and loser only
Victor awarded life to play again, death to the defeated.

Others know only death as the object of the real game.

The true only perceive it to be as part of a new game in physical
death only to start another.

Denying their own existence, the lost in truth of the actual way,
play now as if it were their last.

"Sudden Death" quickens the empty hearts of cowardice.

Clash of the warriors, fool to kill, in his victory the dead has won.

**Baths, bars, the indoor pool. Our injured leader prone on the sweating tile. Chlorine on his breath and in his long hair. Lithe, although crippled, body of a middle-weight contender. Near him the trusted journalist, confidant. He liked men near him with a large sense of life. But most of the press were vultures descending on the curious America aplomb. Cameras inside the coffin interviewing the worms.**

In the realization of the decay, many gasped to the horror but who in reality had pushed for the vision of the known scene? Existing in the coffin, they the curious, felt the quickening in vivid clarity, victims of their own evil plot, each saw their own reflections in destiny, sentenced, withering in final plight.

A connection created in consciousness by a known subconscious thought.

**It takes large murder to turn rocks in the shade and expose strange worms beneath. The lives of our discontented madmen are revealed.**

The killers shrouded in the darkness of black, through young lost eyes, alarm the eagle to the spawn of a generation to come.

**Camera, as all-seeing god, satisfies our longing for omniscience. To spy on others from this height and angle: pedestrians pass in and out of our lens like rare aquatic insects.**

Observed for the induced lesson, awaken the moths from their ethylic slumbers and let them fly.

**Yoga powers. To make oneself invisible or small, to become gigantic and reach to the farthest things, to change the course of nature, to place oneself anywhere in space or time, to summon the dead, to exalt senses and perceive inaccessible images, of events on other worlds, in one's deepest inner mind, or in the minds of others.**

Singular, the homeless retched old man, walks hunched, dragging his bread supply of collected treasures. Mumbling in speech to himself supposed, passerby's laugh in ridicule, mocking his existence. Amid discussions, himself alone, distanced through universe, a friend offers condolences in answer to the voice as the conversation continues.

Crazy old man (?)

**The snipers rifle is an extension of his eye. He kills with injurious vision.**

Sighted in the crosshairs we all wait not knowing when the trigger shall be pulled. Those who pause in the anticipation of what is to come, only stand as easier prey.

**The assassin (?), in flight, gravitated with unconscious, instinctual insect ease, moth-like, toward a zone of safety, haven from the swarming streets. Quickly, he was devoured in the warm, dark, silent maw of the physical theater.**

Wings flutter from the net of the night, drawn by the calling of the believed light. What was once tonic in motion, now resides in a trailed conscious trance, called away from what echoed in warning, through the realms. Snatched by the birds in a loss of innocence to the direction, murderer in row, on line for his execution, awaits the forth coming, darkness.

**Modern circles of Hell: Oswald (?) kills president.**
**Oswald enters taxi. Oswald stops at rooming house.**
**Oswald leaves taxi. Oswald kills Officer Tippitt.**
**Oswald sheds jacket. Oswald is captured.**

**He escaped into a movie house.**

Knight sold souls (?) awakened by society others mock them in difference.
Anger lives.
Cinema gained visions in lieu of reality.
Generations of displacement passed.
Society breeds hate.
Weapons purchased, bombs constructed, instructions obtained from a machine.
Birth to a plan.
Two lone vacant bodies in black enter, automatics sound.
Children and teachers fall to the way amongst the screams.
Blood stains permanent the minds.
Shaped killers, glorified only to themselves in the moment draw upon each other in begotten heroic bliss, they fire.

They learned the scene at a movie house.

**In the womb we are blind Cave Fish.**

Never to know the sun but never more in touch with the riddle of the light, Wrapped in the darkness, supported by a lone cord attached to a given way.

Innocent being, assigned a life of creation, in creation, by the Creator.

**Everything is vague and dizzy. The skin swells and there is no more distinction between parts of body. An encroaching sound of threatening, mocking, monotonous voices, this is fear and attraction of being swallowed.**

Enveloped by what we think we know, lost in the walls, we understand we know nothing of the truth, as the echoing voices become fainter in approach.

Existence comes only in an awareness of the breeze foretold in a beginning whisper by the rustling of all that is around, then felt in a reality as it sweeps over your being to lift one's spirit now connected.

The way is visible only to those who need not to see, for if you must see, in order to know, you never will.

Inside the dream, button sleep around your body like a glove. Free now of space and time, free to dissolve in the streaming summer.

Melted in the warmth of its known comfort, the giver takes away.

**Sleep is an under-ocean dipped into each night. At morning, awake dripping, gasping, eyes stinging,**

**from the sight, in the fire of the sun to the light.**

Reality is real in the seen & unseen, given or not stand true in the direction as a lamb before the Shepard.

In heart, find guidance, in soul, retain comfort, in mind, seek, only spirit.

**The eye looks vulgar inside its ugly shell. Come out in the open in all your brilliance.**

Diffusing the light to make clear the vision, images cast in what is not yet known to exist but known only to be.

Earthly existence is only temporary, being of an existence always, eternal & forever.

**Nothing. The air outside burns my eyes. I'll pull them out and get rid of the burning.**

The sockets left black, harden around the bone. In decaying soil, mouths forever locked open in fear the skull rests, while lying awake.

Blessed with an awareness to know better but most content by having done nothing.

As the Creator beckons in voice, all hear but play deaf in resolve.

Expanded minds locked in idleness. Humanity suffers in a known consciousness as atrophy closes the spectrum of a Universal Being.

The balloon pops!

Existence will cease to channel this plain no more.

Crisp hot whiteness
City Noon
**Occupants of plague zone**
Are consumed.

(Santa Ana's are winds off deserts.)

Rip up grating and splash in gutters.
The search for water, moisture,
"wetness" of the actor, lover.

Softness envelops the hard to open itself up
As the seed to life grows even in dreary dampness
It, will find its way.

Face to the wind let the gust carry away your soul.
Swept from its fleshed covered shell, it is
Forever free to flow.

Spirit in being is like that of the leaf, which has freshly fallen, floating atop a river to show me the way.

Into your hands deliver me unto the Creation!

My being is of your service as servant, not in that of anything of my own.

"Players"—the child, the actor, and the gambler,
the idea of chance is absent from the world of the child and
primitive. The gambler also feels in service of an alien power.
Chance is survival of religion in the modern city, as is theater,
more often cinema, the religion of possession.

The conclusion is in that of the desired thought only, this sent in
mental coded gestures on the final perceived ending to the want,
void of the risks or possibilities encountered. The child, the actor
and gambler...enchant them naive or focused?

**What sacrifice, at what price can the city be born?**

In the wake of the city's new birth, what will it have cost?
The sum is of the whole lost.

There are no longer "dancers," the possessed. The cleavage of men into actor and spectators is the central fact of our time. We are obsessed with heroes who live for us and whom we punish. If all the radios and televisions were deprived of their sources of power, all books and paintings burned tomorrow, all shows and cinemas closed, all the arts of vicarious existence…

Emptied of all the clutter we could return to ourselves.

We are content with the "given" in sensation's quest. We have been metamorphosised from a mad body dancing on hillsides to a pair of eyes staring in the dark.

Blinded in egos of materialistic quests, we will never truly see to exist.

Fool is the fool who horde's his bounty soon, only to have to leave it behind.

Death, "Natures Thief" like a Raven, forever takes the gatherers claim.

Not one of the prisoners regained sexual balance, depressions, impotency, sleeplessness... erotic dispersion, in languages, reading, games, music and gymnastics.

The prisoners built their own theater, which testified to an incredible surfeit of leisure. A young sailor, forced into female roles, soon became the "town" darling, for by this time they called themselves a town, and elected a mayor, police, aldermen.

In the hierarchy of elected officials self-taught, came the harshness in desire, of the coveted whore.

In old Russia, the Czar, each year, granted-out of shrewdness of his own soul or one of his advisors'—a week's freedom for one convict in each of his prisons. The choice was left to the prisoners themselves and it was determined in several ways. Sometimes by vote, sometimes by lot, often by force, it was apparent that the chosen must be a man of magic, virility, experience, perhaps narrative skill, a man of possibility, in short, a hero, impossible selection, defining our world in its percussions.

He, the elected, the viewed Messiah, chosen for an opportunity to a life, must live for a moment even knowing its soon end.

Moment to a memory, make a memory for the moment, for that is all you truly, have.

A room moves over a landscape, uprooting the mind, astonishing vision. A gray film melts off the eyes, and runs down the cheeks. Farewell.

Modern life is a journey by car. The Passengers change terribly in their reeking seats, or roam from car to car, subject to unceasing transformation. Inevitable progress is made toward the beginning (there is no difference in terminals), as we slice through cities, whose ripped backsides present a moving picture of windows, signs, streets, buildings. Sometimes other vessels, closed worlds, vacuums, travel along beside to move ahead or fall utterly behind.

Traveling forward we regress, as the pavement expands and swells to the fattened city. Those stranded as curbside bidders, wave endlessly for a taxi that will never stop.

**Destroy roofs trapped gods, with the gods' omniscient gaze, but without their power to be inside minds and cities as they fly above.**

Unable to view the whole, narrowed by habitual self taught complexities, feathers wilt on wings not used.

Angels fall...

**June 30th. On the sunroof, He woke up suddenly. At that instant a jet from the air base crawled in silence overhead. On the beach, children try to leap into its swift shadow.**

Inching across the vast landscape, a reflection of flight is anchored to the ground.

**The bird or insect that stumbles into a room and cannot find the window because they know no "windows"**

**Wasps, poised in the window, excellent dancers, detached, are not inclined into our chamber.**

**Room of withering mesh read love's vocabulary in the green lamp of tumescent flesh.**

A window closed is never open to what exists on the other side.

Raven and the squirrel together in deed, gathering together out my window collecting the bounty of the harvest in seed.

Cardinal of red, cardinal pale, sing and chase to the day. In opening the window, I can finally hear their song.

**When men conceived buildings, and closed themselves in chambers, first trees and caves.**
**(a window works two ways, mirrors one way.)**
**You never walk through mirrors or swim through windows.**

Round is the circle of the way in life.

A mirror is only a reflection look deeper to see yourself

Stand in a window to see others.

Stare at a mirror to find you.

Return to the caves. Make nests in the trees.

Alive in them no need for mirrors or windows.

All is equal in equal to all.

**Cure blindness with a whore's spittle.**

For in her, those with sight gave it away.

**In Rome, Prostitutes were exhibited on roofs above the public highways for the dubious hygiene of loose tides of men whose potential lust endangered the fragile order of power. It is even reported that patrician ladies, masked and naked, sometimes offered themselves up to these deprived eyes for private excitements of their own.**

The lure of the erotic is often a pathway led from the exotic. In the excitement of the forbidden comes the same titillation of biting the apple hung before you but created wrong by thought, one seeks in curiosity, to just know.

More or less, we're all afflicted with the psychology of the voyeur. Not in a strictly clinical or criminal sense, but in our whole physical and emotional stance before the world. Whenever we seek to break this spell of passivity, our actions are cruel and awkward and generally obscene, like an invalid, who has forgotten how to walk.

Struggling within our selves forever off balance, in mental conflict, we naturally seek but are taught to turn away.

The voyeur, the peeper, the Peeping Tom, is a dark comedian. He is repulsive in his dark anonymity, in his secret invasion. He is pitifully alone. But strangely, he is able through this same silence and concealment to make unknowing partner of anyone within his eye's range. This is his threat and power. There are no glass houses. The shades are drawn and "real" life begins. Some activities are impossible in the open. And these secret events are the voyeur's game. He seeks them out with his myriad army of eyes—like the child's notion of a Deity who sees all. "Everything?" asks the child. "Yes, everything," they answer, and the child is left to cope with this divine intrusion.

Control the thought, control the action, control the mind, if allowed, it can only change.

Play child play, soon innocence will be lost to the ways of growth, self-inflicted by learned control. Enforced by the "Watcher" a mere voyeur on patrol who exercises restraint upon the mind, implanting secondary conceptions into all thoughts once that of your own.

**The voyeur is masturbator, the mirror his badge, the window his prey.**

Wrapped up in a mindset, enslaved by instinct, drawn to the curiosity of possibility, open to the motivation but entranced by a society he so largely disarms but cannot accept, he views to cast judgment but in apparent decline does nothing. The match burns held in the fingers of a civilization, uncivil. "OZ" is just a man behind the curtain.

Voyeurism, Idealness, a society content to watch, itself sleep as the Beast Dragon is released from the sea.

Blood soon to stain the sand.

"Holy War," Unholy.

**Urge to come to terms with the "Outside," by absorbing, interiorizing it. I won't come out, you must come in to me. Into my womb-garden where I peer out. Where I can construct a universe within the skull, to rival the real.**

Take this step to release back out what is absorbed in you, grown in the soil of self, then catered to the existence around, let it all go to really be.

**She said, "Your eyes are always black." The pupil opens to seize the object of vision.**

Locked in an image to the sight, focus through the darkness to understand the light.

The eye is a mirror to all souls reflecting the image of existence in an empty blank nothingness, all can be found.

He said, "You see in my eye's reflection only black as I view it all."

**Imagery is born of loss. Loss of the "friendly expanses." The breast is removed and the face imposes its cold, curious, forceful, and inscrutable presence.**

Among the disparity of a culture crying, stands the innocence in smile of a lone child.

**You may enjoy life from afar. You may look at things but not taste them. You may caress the mother only with the eyes.**

Neutral to the balance, centered at the pole, reserves the commitments of reaching for an end.

But in this life has a life lived?

No faults in seeking.

Growth is the only thing to be gained.

The apple is present in sight only when viewed for the first time. It is not until it is touched that it can be felt. It is not until it is bitten that it can be tasted. It is not until it is swallowed that it's meaning for existence is found.

Now, once personally known, all can be realized through thought only. The apple no longer needs to be seen in order to see it. No longer bitten in order to be tasted. No longer swallowed for its reason to be understood.

God is the same.

Exist to be a part of all but first reach out to what all exists.

Touch Life, Taste the World, Swallow in the Universe to Understand.

**You cannot touch these phantoms.**

Forever attached, they are bound by what you cannot grasp, yet you alone hold them.

**French Deck. Solitary stroker of cards. He dealt himself a hand. Turn stills of the past in unending permutations, shuffle and begin. Sort the images again. And sort them again. This game reveals germs of truth, and death.**

The world becomes an apparently infinite, yet possibly finite, card game. Image combinations, permutations, comprise the world game.

Study your adversary, the "Dealer of Life" play your hand wisely not in reckless care. Win to gather the rewards. Lose, shuffle and play again.

**A mild possession, devoid of risk, at bottom sterile with an image there is no attendant danger.**

The blades edge is harmless until it is touched. Existence is easy until it is lived.

Develop perception.

Place your finger upon the blades edge but in learned wisdom know that it can cut.

**Muybridge derived his animal subjects from the Philadelphia Zoological Garden, Male performers from the University. The women were professional artists' models, also actresses and dancers, parading nude before the 48 cameras.**

Brought in focus to the scope of the master eye, merely a puppeteer, walking his subjects lifeless, connected by string only in a manner to which he envisions—"The Director" controls all that are bound to the control.

**Films are collections of dead pictures, which are given artificial insemination.**

Frame by frame, the moment is brought to life only to be viewed at another time. Cast onto a screen in projection of a light not truly of the same.

**Film spectators are quiet vampires.**

Draining from the pictured thoughts of another they feed themselves, digest and leave, parasitic in nature, self-serving.

**Cinema is most totalitarian of the arts. All energy and sensation is sucked up into the skull, a cerebral erection, skull bloated with blood. Caligula wished a single neck for all his subjects that he could behead a kingdom with one blow. Cinema is this transforming agent. The body exists for the sake of the eyes; it becomes a dry stalk to support these two soft insatiable jewels.**

Through them all perceptions encase mental images, "snapshot" photographs of an encoded sight, related the brain retrieves the picture.

Most of a cinema cast plot from someone else's thought. The scene from a movie we remember, locked forever to a spot. What image does the blind man see? Sightless from birth, forever in darkness, knowing only the sensation of shadows and light, retrieving his images only in shapes given from the night?

**Film confers a kind of spurious eternity.**

Brooke like, in the channel of a channel lie's another channel. Forever moving, one can never step back into the real existing same, but only yet another part of.

A captured moment to show forever, film transfers by picture, a past moment now transferred to the present, each time it is viewed that recorded portal exists again to that concurrent time now new but also a part of before.

Each film depends upon all the others and drives you on to others. Cinema was a novelty, a scientific toy, until a sufficient body of works had been amassed, enough to create an intermittent other world, a powerful, infinite mythology to be dipped into at will.

Films have an illusion of timelessness fostered by their regular, indomitable appearance.

The element essential for modern cinemas success is its inane ability to transport the viewer audience minds in "wholeness" through portals of time, in a separate dimension of conceived thought perceptions. Einstein smiles, "Is time travel possible in relativity, if all is relative?" "Yes", he answers himself, "Through film and screen, forward or back."

**The appeal of cinema lies in the fear of death.**

We know that the film, play, life, will at some point end. The self-asked wonderment is in the how? Thus all seek in drawn curiosity, to the answer of the unknown end.

**The modern East creates the greatest body of films. Cinema is a new form of an ancient tradition-the shadow play. Even their theater is an imitation of it. Born in India or China, the shadow show was aligned with religious ritual, linked with celebrations, which centered around, cremation of the dead.**

The masters in one continuous stroke, spoke of the way long lost, in a wiseness to creation born of the existence, begot of their virtues, stolen from the ventricles of their hearts, in ashes released to the winds, forever blows the spirit of life.

**It is wrong to assume, as some have done, that cinema belongs to women, cinema, is created by men, for the consolation of men.**

The female by creation superior, yet content, does not feed herself on quests of Bravo image self. The male, amid his denied secondary, creates false attachments for ego, to prove his wanted superiority. In sexual gender, cinema fulfills this for the male, as the damsel, a maiden so fair, is cut away from the tracks. The gallant hero, just in time, removes her swooning from the pathway of the forthcoming train. The villain again foiled, awaits another day.

**The shadow plays originally were restricted to male audiences. Men could view these dream shows from either side of the screen. When women later began to be admitted, they were allowed to attend only to shadows.**

The female placed separate again secondary but believed correct, a choice made by man soulful on esoteric ego's, holding off the given balance, the plaque of our continued existence.

**Male genitals are small faces forming trinities of thieves and Christ's Fathers, sons, and ghosts.**
**A nose hangs over a wall and two half eyes, sad eyes, mute and handless, multiply an endless round of victories.**
**These dry and secret triumphs, fought in stalls and stamped in prisons, glorify our walls and scorch our vision.**
**A horror of empty spaces propagates this seal on private places.**

Primitive of urge, driven by instinct, the faces change in the movement, full only in blood as the seeker rises again, only for the self-gain. Chemically driven insane on function, slave to the body, Man… unable to conquer his own self w/ a given superior brain.

"Fuck It or Kill It, Fuck It or Kill It, Fuck It or Kill It…"

**Kynaston's Bride**
**May not appear**
**But the odor of her flesh**
**Is never very far. I**
**Fragrant amenities afloat the stormy sky,**
**Kindle ancient swellings within loins of flesh.**

Twisted locked in unity, the couple reach to the calling
Atop, the lover stained, cloth.
Release awaken,
I am alone.

**A drunken crowd knocked over the apparatus, and Mayhew's showman, exhibiting at Islington Green, burned up, with his mate, inside.**

Tragedy amongst the arts strikes quick, birthing new art in a line created,
As all too soon, the movie is cast.

**In 1832,Gropius was astounding Paris with his Pleorama. The audience was transformed into a crew aboard a ship engaged in battle. Fire, screaming, sailors, drowning.**

The playwright was victorious in quest through words and motion he transcended set limitations. Grasping the audience now lifted unto his motivation, placing them in mind amongst the scene of a created setting, supposed now real in thought, the spectators, like the actors, looking to escape in helpless generated emotion, squirm in their seats to a cast anxiety.

Robert Baker, an Edinburgh artist, while in jail for debt, was struck by the effect of light shining through the bars of his cell through a letter he invented the first panorama, a concave, transparent picture view of the city.

This invention was soon replaced by the Diorama, which added the illusion of movement by shifting the room. Also sounds and novel lighting effects, Daguerre's London Diorama still stands in Regents Park, a rare survival, since these shows depended always on effects of artificial light, produced by lamps or gas jets, and nearly end, in fire.

In captive stillness, the creator created, through mindlessness, he stumbled onto what was always there. Everything invented is not new but only then discovered.

Phanasmagoria, magic lantern shows, spectacles without substance. They achieved complete sensory experiences through noise, incense, lighting & water. There may be a time when we'll attend Weather Theaters to recall the sensation of rain.

Sad be the day when numb tears fall, for we know not why we cry.

Cinema has evolved in two paths.

One is spectacle. Like the Phantasmagoria, its goal is the creation of a total substitute sensory world.

The other is peep show, which claims for its realm both the erotic and the untampered observance of real life, and imitates the keyhole or voyeur's window without need of color, noise or grandeur.

Loath the day when cinema's pathways cross and its audience, reflected in screen, is no longer separate in paths considered then the "norm."

Real life today is demanded in spectacle, "American Beauty" accepted madness, society's fall.

**Cinema discovers its fondest affinities, not with painting, literature, or theatre, but with the popular diversions-comics, chess, French and Tarot decks, magazines, and tattooing.**

Dazzled in his magic, the magician casts the illusion while the gypsy views the scene through her ball.

Cinema derives not from painting, literature, sculpture, theater, but from ancient popular wizardry. It is the contemporary manifestation of an evolving history of shadows, a delight in pictures that move, a belief in magic. Its lineage is entwined from the earliest beginning with priests and sorcery, a summoning of phantoms. With, at first, only slight aid of mirror and fire, men called up dark and secret visits from regions in the buried mind. In these séances, shades are spirits, which ward off evil.

Demons conjured of illusion, created in art, fall prey to the Jackals as the mystic Gargoyles return to their perch's of stone.

Alive in theater, in unseen darkness, lurks the life of the night. Brought to vision in a created thought, projected to the masses, seemingly illuminated, to be physically real.

In the séance, the shaman led. A sensuous panic, deliberately evoked through drugs, chants, dancing, hurls the shaman into trance. Changed voice, convulsive movement, He, acts, like a madman. These professional hysterics, chosen precisely for their psychotic leaning, were once esteemed. They meditated between man and spirit-world. Their mental travels formed the crux of the religious life of the tribe.

Entranced with unity, lost but not far, the "Channeler's" probe is opened to connect, retrieving what the ancients all know to be.

"Comeback my children wondering in the way."

Strange, fertile correspondences the alchemists sensed in unlikely orders of being. Between men and planets, plants and gestures, words and weather. These disturbing connections: an infant's cry and the stroke of silk; the whorl of an ear and an appearance of dog's in the yard; a woman's head lowered in sleep and the morning dance of cannibals; these are conjunctions which transcend the sterile signal of any "willed" montage. These juxtapositions of objects, sounds, actions, colors, weapons, wounds, and odors shine in an unheard-of-way, impossible ways.

Film is nothing when not an illumination of this chain of being which makes a needle poised in flesh call up explosions in a foreign capital.

Polaris intense, as the ice shifts, rocks align in planetary slumber. All things not connected are, the moon rises into the night as the waves crash against the shore.

**Cinema returns us to anima, religion of matter, which gives each thing its special divinity and sees gods in all things and beings.**

**Cinema, heir of alchemy, last of an erotic science.**

Born of pleasure, lost in conscience, adrift the descending fall, we ride the communal wave.

The theory is that birth is prompted by the child's desire to leave the womb. But in the photograph an unborn horse's neck strains inward w/ legs scooped out.
From this everything follows:
Swallow milk at the breast until there's no milk.
Squeeze wealth at the rim until tile pools claim it.
He swallows seed, his pride until with pale mouth legs she sucks the root, dreading world to devour child.
Doesn't the ground swallow me when I die, or the sea if I die at sea?

Devouring only to be devoured in turn. Parasites to the landscape Texas scene: Man crafted mosquito's of bolt and steel, suck up the mothers rich black blood as she grows weary, sourced in auto by the ants, in faithful service to the unseen Queen. The Jester dances a fool before the fools.

The City. Hive, Web, or severed insect mound. All citizens' heirs of the same royal parent. The caged beast, the holy center, a garden in the midst of the city.

"See Naples & die." Jump ship. Rats, sailors & death.
So many wild pigeons & animals ripe w/ new diseases. "There is only one disease and I am its catalyst," cried doomed pride of the carrier.
Fighting, dancing, gambling, bars, cinemas thrive in the avid summer.

Intricate parts of the inner mound thus created, the Colony, our kingdom, the City's fumes choke off the life force of the given existence. Traffic Ants aligned to known pathways sit locked, striving to deliver with restlessness, morsel's found along the way, donated in a life, to maintain the infinite appetite of the unknown Queen they serve, "Ruler to The Lords" of a lost created being. The Virus spreads.

"Mankind" the plague of all plague's. Enlightened to the intelligence by evolution, to see it's own wrong, yet overall, unwilling to change in order to correct the understood error.

**The spectator is a dying animal.**

A head on shoulders, faceless among the vast crowd, living a connection through idols on a field, they gaze in wonder as bystanders of an inflicted, "Worldly Way" content to only watch, as the game to an existence is being lost.

**Invoke, palliate & drive away the Dead. Nightly.**

For they come knocking in the slumber of the open black.
The Devil's dance in the subconscious thought.
Entering the open areas like roaches in darkness,
they commune,
only to scatter in the presence of the light.

**Through ventriloquism, gestures, play with objects, and all rare variations of the body in space, the shaman signaled his "trip" to an audience, which shared the journey.**

Let the lesson begin, in united fronts calling up from that which is within, forever in contact knowing all that is around, "Hello," says a familiar voice.

Principal of séance: to cure illness. A mood might overtake a people burdened by historical events or dying in a bad landscape. They seek deliverance from doom, death & dread. Seek possession, the visit of gods and powers, a rewining of the life source from demon possessors. The cure is culled from ecstasy. Cure illness or prevent its visit, revive the sick and regain stolen soul.

Avoid the cancer in "Ego of Self," remain to the pure. Serve to help only, not to prosper in intent from the misfortunes of others. Simple is the path, good for the good, not of the gain.

**It is wrong to assume that art needs the spectator in order to be. The film runs on without any eyes. The spectator cannot exist without it. It insures his existence. A constant reaffirmation to life, in its absence he would surely die.**

(yet another victim of Hollywood)

Lost is the soul who cannot find a single reason to live but the arts will continue to exist in and of its self, alone, not searching for any reason.

The happening/ the event in which ether is introduced into a roomful of people through air vents makes the chemical an actor. Its agent, or injector, is an artist-showman who creates a perform-ance to witness himself. The people consider themselves audience, while they perform for each other, and the gas acts out poems of its own through the medium of the human body. This approaches the psychology of the orgy while remaining in the realm of the Game and its infinite permutations.

The aim of the happening is to cure boredom. Wash the eyes make childlike reconnections with the stream of life. Its lowest, widest aim is for the purgation of perception. The happening attempts to engage all the senses, the total orgasm, and achieve total response in the face of traditional arts, which focus on nar-rower inlets of sensation.

Cinema, the movie, in proper structure and context to an emo-tion, enlightens all senses through multi-stimulation via approach, shock, twist or thought, cast over the people in spell like form, the spectators entranced to the stimuli.... Come.

**Multimedias are invariably sad comedies. They work as a kind of colorful group therapy, a woeful mating of actors and viewers, a mutual semi-masturbation. The performers seem to need their audience and the spectators-the spectators would find these same mild titillations in a freak show or fun fair and fancier, more complete amusements in a Mexican cathouse.**

As the entities are joined, unfulfilled, yet aroused, they seek even more stimuli from the arts in an orgasmic quest, fed from the perplexed illuminations of the artists themselves. Both parties, mating each other for the gratification of themselves as the audience needs an actor and the actor more importantly, needs the audience. Unsatisfied in climax to their coupling, not gratified, hungry for more, each seeks out yet another joining, as the writer sells his next script.

**Novices, we watch the moves of silkworms who, excite their bodies in moist leaves and weave wet nests of hair and skin. This is a model of our liquid resting world dissolving bone and melting marrow, opening pores as wide as windows.**

Soft is the water that breaks up the rock, longing to be still it journeys, searching only for a place of rest.
Wise ancients have always spoken.

**The "Stranger" was sensed as greatest menace in ancient communities.**

Fearful of all that was not known about him, yet in truth, a group more akin to the emotion in desire, to be more like him in what people did not know.

**Metamorphose. An object is cut off from its name, habits, associations detached it becomes only the thing, in and of itself. When this disintegration into pure existence is at last achieved, the object is free to become endlessly anything.**

"Who named the Bear?" Asked the young child. "I don't know?" Said the man. "What was it called before it was named?" Again, asked the child. "Brother!" said the man. "God did not name it?" Puzzled, the boy asked. "I don't believe so?" Said the man. " And who was God before his name?" The child demanded. "A part of you!" Softly, the man answered.

**The subject says, " I see first lots of things which dance...then everything becomes gradually connected."**

In bliss lives the being void of senses, in his emptiness lives the harmony of all.

**Objects as they exist in time the clean eye and camera, give us. Not falsified by "seeing."**

Void of prejudice in unlearned thought, it develops the true and recounts in a moment, the actual sight.

**When there are as yet no objects.**

True peace exists.

Genius is the fool, content in their own misgivings of what they cannot understand to judge.

**Early filmmakers, who-like the alchemists-delighted in a willful obscurity about their craft, in order to withhold their skills from profane onlookers.**

**Separate, purify, reunite the formula of Ars Magna, and its heir, the cinema.**

**The camera is androgynous machine, a kind of mechanical hermaphrodite.**

Both male and female, it captures the whole. Identifiable w/ parts of each, it exists separate.

**In his retort the alchemist repeats the work of Nature.**

Singing with the frogs as they return from their mud dwelled slumber. Calling into the darkness for a life to come.

Few would defend a small view of Alchemy as "Mother of Chemistry," and confuse its true goal with those external metal arts. Alchemy is an erotic science, involved in buried aspects of reality, aimed at purifying and transforming all being and matter. Not to suggest that material operations are ever abandoned. The adept holds both the mystical and physical work.

"Did you hear me?" whispered, the voice.
"Did you see me?" said, the vision.
"Did you think?" asked, the thought.
"No!" said, the wise.
"I just knew."

The alchemists detect in sexual activity of man a correspondence with the world's creation, with the growth of plants, and with mineral formations. When they see the union of rain and earth, they see it in an erotic sense, as copulation. And this extends to all natural realms of matter. For they can picture love affairs of chemicals and stars, a romance of stones, or the fertility of fire.

Life breeds life, in an internal driven quest. All extending, for the reception of another, in the continued universal orgy, that is our present existence.

**Surround emperor of Body.**
**Bali Bali dancers**
**Will not break my temple.**
**Explorers suck eyes into the head.**
**The rosy body cross**
**Secret in flow controls its flow.**
**Wrestlers in body weights dance and music, mimesis, body.**
**Swimmers entertain embryo sweet dangerous thrust flow.**

Politicians, charmers of the plight lead the people from the light.
Child, born of peace made murderer to the greed,
Daughter taken of innocence ripped of her seed.

The Lords. Events take place beyond our knowledge or control. Our lives are lived for us. We can only try to enslave others. But gradually, special perceptions are being developed. The idea of the "Lords" is beginning to form in some minds we should enlist them into bands of perceivers to tour the labyrinth during mysterious nocturnal appearances. The Lords have secret entrances, and they know disguises. But they give themselves away in minor ways. Too much glint of light in the eye. A wrong gesture too long and curious a glance.

The Lords appease us with images. They give us books, concerts, galleries, shows, cinemas, especially the cinemas. Through art they confuse us and blind us to our enslavement. Art adorns our prison walls, keeps us silent and diverted and indifferent.

The Lords encase control upon the masses w/ no control. Amongst the chaos and disorder, lies the silent orders' of the order.

The new revolution is priming in the girth of a mother of generations lost. Spawned in the excesses of excess.

Children of a media numbed plot grow discontent.

**Snakeskin jacket**
**Indian eyes**
**Brilliant hair**

**He moves in disturbed**
**Nile insect**
**Air**

Cautious wisdoms
Countless
Fair

Walking the journey
On endless
Dare

Free of possessions
He would not
Bare

**You parade through the soft summer**
**We watch your eager rifle decay**
**Your wilderness**
**Your teeming emptiness**
**Pale forests on verge of light**
**Decline.**

**More of your miracles**
**More of your magic arms**

Wrap them around us
To begin the healing
Hold the children born of your being

Attach them to your breast to again teach them the way

Dull lions prone on a watery beach.
The universe kneels at the swamp
To curiously eye its own raw
Postures of decay
In the mirror of human consciousness.
Absent and peopled mirror, absorbent,
Passive to whatever visits
And retains its interest.
Door of passage to the other side,
The soul frees itself in stride.
Turn to the wall
In the house of the new dead.

Cast, in a reflection, look beyond
The image.
See through the known existence,
In true vastness,
The journey begins through the
Eyes, to find the soul,
Closed, or open the Spirit is always there.

**Bitter grazing in sick pastures animal sadness and the daybed whipping.**
**Iron curtains pried open. The elaborate sun implies dust, knives, voices.**
**Call out of the wilderness**
**Call out of the fever,**
**receiving the wet dreams of an Aztec King.**

Who now resounds in festive plume, standing w/ a blood drenched dagger atop the masses.

He raises the Virgins heart still beating, innocent, never to know love.

**The banks are high & overgrown**
**Rich w/ warm green danger.**
**Unlock the canals.**
**Punish our sister's sweet playmate distress.**
**Do you want us that way with the rest?**
**Do you adore us?**
**When you return will you still want to play w/ us?**

I think not.

Controlled by our own order.

The True Creator, God, has been
Reformed, in misleading man-crafted conceptions, created by an
empty ploy to real faith.

The church, once holy, now stained in the blood of worldly greed.

Created weak in its own existence, tarnished in misdirection by
self-serving souls.

The simplicity in all that was to be has been lost.

Fall down.
Strange gods arrive in fast enemy poses.
Their shirts are soft marrying cloth and hair together.
All along their arms ornaments conceal vein bluer than blood
Pretending welcome. Soft lizard eyes connect.
Their soft drained insect cries erect
New fear, where fears reign,
The rustling of sex against their skin.
The wind withdraws all sound.
Stamp your witness on the punished ground.

Conception complete.
In fragile egg, the embryos form their reptilian armor.
Encompassed in a life not yet served.
Destiny already given,
Existence belongs to those not yet born but lived in the deeds of
the past.

Wounds, stags, & arrows
Hooded flashing legs plunge near the tranquil women.
Startling obedience from the pool of people.
Astonishing caves to plunder.
Loose, nerveless ballets of looting.
Boys are running.
Girls are screaming, falling.
The air is thick w/ smoke.
Dead crackling wires dance pools of sea blood.

The serpents long restrained by the ancient journeymen
Are released. Uncoiling in slither,
As the snow caps, break.
Families lie huddled
In a crouched embrace
Praying, to the Creator but afraid to face.

Lizard Woman w/ your insect eyes w/ your wild surprise.
Warm daughter of silence. Venom.
Turn your back w/ a slither of moaning wisdom.
Behind walls new histories rise and wake
Growling & whining the weird dawn of dreams.
Dogs lie sleeping. The wolf howls.
A creature lives out the war.
A forest.
A rustle of cut words, choking river.

In your journey to vastness,
Shrinking in atrophy from
The brook.
Lizard Woman, alive she cries,
Lost in the doom
She tears at her eyes.
Visions not changing stranded
Helpless, as the cure dies.

The snake, the lizard, the insect eye
The huntsman's green obedience.
Quick, in raw time, serving
Grinding warm forests into restless lumber.

Now for the valley.
Now for the syrup hair.
Stabbing the eyes, widening skies
Behind the skull bone.
Swift end of hunting.
Hug round the swollen torn breast
And red stained throat.
The hounds gloat.
Take her home.
Carry our sister's body, back
To the boat.

Created in harmony, taken of peace.
A casualty of order, swung lifeless
Over the victor's shoulder,
Fear locked limbs swing to
The sway
Gentle eye's open, never again too
See the day.

**A pair of wings**
**Crash**
**High winds of karma**

**Sirens**

**Laughter and young voices**
**In the mountains.**

Forsaken lovers run
Naked
Through a field of wild
Flowers

The hawk circles
Crying
To the Spirit

Again the sirens

Lone raven leaps
As the
Branch rises

Distant is the
Sound
Of thunder

Angered Spirits
Rumble
The intent

**Saints**
**The Negro, Africa**
**Tatoo**
**Eyes like time**

Open but weary,

Ancients guard the
Secrets of the Dogma,

Wise to count the knots
On their sacred, strands.

Build temporary habitations, games
& chambers, play there, hide.

First man stood, shifting stance
While germs of sight
Unfurled flags in his skull

And quickening, hair, nails, skin
Turned slowly, whirled, in
The warm aquarium, warm
Wheel turning.

Cave fish, eels, & gray salamanders
Turn in their night career of sleep.

The idea of vision escapes
The animal worm whose earth
Is an ocean, whose eye is its body.

The mole sightless from birth to the light,
but who can still see the way.

Non-content in restless dwelling,
Man, in his own arrogance,
Supposed, superior.

Places himself in order
Above the Primates who
Showed him the way.

Humankind, consumed in its own intelligence,
Denies, it's one given chance.

**Savage destiny**
**Naked girl, seen from behind,**
**On a natural road**
**Friends**
**Explore the labyrinth**
**-Movie**
**Young woman left on the desert**
**A city gone mad w/ fever**

Seekers now lost in the ivy,
Walk changing amid the circle.
As the girl from the desert enters,

At peace in its center, two lovers lay
Resting, head atop the maidens
Nest, safely wrapped between her
Legs, the journeyman sleeps.

Sisters of the unicorn, dance
Sisters & brothers of Pyramid
Dance

Mangled hands
Tales of the old Days
Discovery of the Sacred Pool
Changes
Mute-handed stillness baby cry

The wild dog
The sacred beast

Find her!

The Virgin in white skins of
Leather, stands before
The coming.

Seven virtues she taught,
Have fallen.

Twice in attempt to
offer the salvation,
Led by the sacred
Watanka, denied.

Slain again, by the Blue Man,
Throat cut, the foretold brother
Bleeds.

Hope for a civilization dies among
The early spring grasses of a
Mid-west prairie.

He goes to see the girl
Of the ghetto.
Dark savage streets.
A hut, lighted by candle.
She is magician
Female prophet
Sorceress
Dressed in the past
All arrayed.

The stars the moon
She reads the future
In your hand.

Full of the supposed coming
Days, he seeks to fulfill its
Truths laid forth
On the words of a teller.

Directions cast before him
By a stranger.

**The walls are garish red**
**The stairs**
**High discordant screaming**
**She has the tokens.**
**"You too"**
**"Don't go"**
**he flees.**
**Music renews.**

**The mating-pit.**
**"Salvation"**
**Tempted to leap in circle.**

**Negroes riot.**

Streets burn in the violence
Taught from a whip long
Ago.

No longer chained but
Still bound.

They seek the vengeance of
a prosecutor no longer
living in body but alive
among the majority, in imposed
misconceptions.

A bigger threat to all.

**Fear the Lords who are secret among us.**
**As the Lords dwell within us.**
**Born of sloth & cowardice.**

They lurk in the shadows of all mankind.
Everyone is victim to a second self,
Do not let them rule!

**He spoke to me. He frightened**
**Me w/ laughter. He took**
**My hand, & led me past**
**Silence into cool whispered bells.**

Amongst the chimes I saw
The beginning to that
Which has no end.

**A file of young people**
**Going thru a small woods**

Led by the Witch who works for "The Lords".
Into the night, she dances naked in
Swirls, before them.
Body entrancing, heightened
By the moons glow, casting pleasurable
Shadows, of the forbidden.
Stoned in her beauty, the youths
Are lost in worldly, flesh hardened desires,
Unable to break free of her spell, they follow her stoned
Unto the existing, doom.

**They are filming something**
**In the street, in front of our house.**

"Look @ the crowd gather!"
"What could it be?"
"Why do I feel so funny?"
"What's w/ all the people & cameras?"
"What's happening now?"
"I can't see."
"What's with that light?"
"Please excuse me?"
"Why all the commotion?"
"A man has been shot?"
"Who?"
"Where are the police?"
"Where are the paramedics?"
"Oh my God!"
" What if it's someone I know?"
"Hey!"
"Let me see who it is?"
"Please, I live here!"
"Stand back!"
"Where did they shoot him?"
"Once in the head & twice in the chest?"
"Who are you by the way?"
"What do you mean?"
"Why is this man dead?"
"What?" They killed him just because he lived here?"
"But I…"

**Walking to the riot**
**Spreads to the houses the lawns**
**Suddenly alive now w/**
**People running**

Others fall victim to the club,
As they are trotted down before
The advancing shields,
Beaten by the "Protectors Of The People,"
clad in full armor.

Canister's hiss expelling
their fume, as the Blue Man, over Cocktails,
shakes hands w/ the leader of "The Lords".

Humanity sentenced…

Rain falls as the sky weeps.

I don't dig what they did
To that girl
Mercy Pack
Wild song they sing
As they chop her hands
Nailed to a ghost
Tree

I saw a lynching
Met the strange men
Of the swamp
Cypress was their talk
Fish-call & bird-song
Roots & signs
Out of all knowing
They chanced to be there
Guides, to the white
Gods.

The pupil, a poet, w/
Ink and pad writes omega
To the spirit dancers
Chained to the night.

Linked in harmony to the land,
Abound around, overcast in the neon,
All are blocked from the sound.

**An armed camp.**
**Army army**
**Burning itself in**
**Feasts.**

Drunken in said Christian splendor,
The soldier's anxiously wait turn.
The Croatian child, a girl, no more then thirteen,
Torn prior, numbed by the numbers,
She drifts from her being as another
Mounts.

"These are the people of the Christ?" She, whispers.

"They are not of me!" Softly answers a voice.

Jackal, we sniff after the survivors of caravans.
We reap bloody crops on war fields.
No meat of any corpse deprives our lean bellies.
Hunger drives us on scented winds.
Stranger, traveler,
Peer into our eyes & translate
The horrible barking of ancient dogs.

Born scavengers, to search a continued nomadic existence.
Wondering, we howl into the night to communicate w/
our brethren, distanced only in realms of perceived
Worlds.

All more related then we care to acknowledge, being is led one by
the other.

Damness to soul, self-inflicted

**Camel caravans bear
Witness guns to Cesar.
Hordes crawl & seep inside
The walls. The streets
Flow stone. Life goes
On absorbing war. Violence
Kills the temple of no sex.**

Barren in the travesty to man led religions
Is the evils to all?
More have been slain
In the name of the cross,
Then those of faith care
To remember.

Nations and tribes, in worship of idols,
Chant to their created entities and rot from within
Their own misleading tithes.

**Terrible shouts start**
**The journey**
**if they had migrated sooner**

**a high wailing keening**
**piercing animal lament**
**from a woman**
**high atop a Mt. Tower**

**Thin wire fence**
**in the mind**
**dividing the heart**

In barren bliss,
The mother cries
Fluids of life stream down
her thighs.

voice within the soul

hear me

Travel in mind to the heavens,
Recant the demons,
Lift up the dawn.

Surreptitiously
They smile
Inventing-smiling
Choktai
Leave!
Evil
No come here
Leave her!

A creature is nursing
Its child
Soft arms around
The head & the neck
A mouth to connect
Leave this child alone
This one is mine
I'm taking her home
Back to the rain

Torn from its mothers breast
Still feeding. The chosen
Infant of the forest,


Marked for destiny by the
Ancients,
Is returned back to the trees.

**The assassin's bullet**
**Marries the king**
**Dissembling miles of air**
**To kiss the crown.**
**The prince rambles in blood.**
**Ode to the neck**
**That was groomed**
**For rape's gown.**

The marked must
Assume the chair.
Directed since birth,
Born inherited to the task,
Not by choice,
Right of the throne.

**Cancer city**
**urban fall**
**Summer sadness**
**the highways of the old town**
**Ghosts in cars,**
**electric shadows**

Pass with the empty train.
Corners stand lifeless,
as darkened rainbows of hope
fade through the slithering film which flows @ the
edge of the streets,
soon only to fall through
the drains.

**Ensenada**
**The dead seal**
**The dog crucifix**
**Ghosts of the dead car sun.**
**Stop the car.**
**Rain. Night.**
**Feel.**

Hear the drum,
Call to the clouds.
Answer the ancients,
Worship only God
Praise Jehovah
Thank the Spirit.
Return with peace.

**Sea-bird sea-moon**
**Earthquake murmuring**
**Fast-burning incense**
**Clamoring surging**
**Serpentine road**
**To the Chinese caves**
**Home of the winds**
**The gods of mourning**

Gaze touch the ancestors,
Dance outstretched,
Breath in the universe,
Take in no breath.
Earth, my mother,
Teach me the way of worthy,
In the night, to your call,
I listen.

The city sleeps
As the unhappy children
roam w/ animal gangs.
They seem to speak
To their friends
The dogs
Who teach them trails.
Who can catch them?
Who can make them come
Inside?

Instant wealth and grander
beckons to the nibblers
of the crumbs.
In hunger they join the pack to
survive. Roaming the boundaries
on all fours,
"Wolves Of The Ghetto"
Praying on their own kind,
in cannibalistic survival.

"The Lords" in the streets breathe fire.

Placed in blood by a needle, trapped in breath by the pipe.

**The tent girl**
**at midnight**
**stole to the well**
**& met her lover there.**

First son, "Heir to the Tribe."

**They talked a while**
**& laughed**
**& then he left,**
**she put an orange pillow**
**on her breast.**

**In the morning**
**Chief withdrew his troops**
**& planned a map.**
**The horsemen rose on up,**
**the women fixed the ropes**
**on tight.**
**The tents are folded now,**
**we march toward the sea.**

The tent girl,
orange pillow still
clutched to her breast,
stepped light in the

glow of love
among the servants.
Dreaming in pleasure
& fancy she
followed the rest.

Caressed in a forbidden
tale to a promised
future
never to be.

Captive to words spoken
not true but used to
obtain.

Pillow to her bosom,
blinded of the reality,
clasping all that she will ever truly,
hold.

**Catalog of Horrors**
**Descriptions of Natural disaster**
**Lists of miracles in the divine corridor**
**Catalog of objects in the room**
**List of things in the sacred river.**

Charted among the "Scrolls to Life"
In the register of "Saved Souls."
The Chancellor, frantically searched
for his own inscription.

"What are you doing?" demanded, the Voice.

"I'm searching for my name!" In panic, the man shouted.

"If you have to look, it will not be there." Came, the stern reply.

1

The soft parade has now begun
On Sunset.
Cars come thundering down
The canyon.
Now is the time & the place.
The cars come rumbling.
"You got a cool machine."
These engine beasts
Muttering their soft
Talk. A delight
At night
To hear they're quiet voices
Again
After 2 years.

Now the soft parade
Has soon begun.
Cool pools
From a tired land
Sink now
In the peace of evening.

Clouds weaken
& die.

The sun, an orange skull,
Whispers quietly, becomes an
Island, & is gone.

There they are
Watching
us everything
will be dark.
The light changed.
We were aware
Knee-deep in the fluttering air
As the ships move on
Trains in their wake.
Trench mouth
Again in the camps.
Gonorrhea
Tell the girl to go home
We need a witness
To the killing.

One lone child
Stands powerless
Before the masses,


Mother enslaved,
Father not known,
Messiah thought absent.
The sword is raised,
While the tribesmen begin
To chant,
As the chosen
Cries out to the trees.

ll

The artist of Hell
Set up easels in parks
The terrible landscape,
Where citizens find anxious pleasure
Preyed upon by savage bands of youths

I can't believe this is happening
I can't believe all these people
Are sniffing each other
And backing away
Teeth grinning
Hair raised, growling, here in
The slaughtered wind

I am ghost killer.
Witnessing to all
My blessed sanction
This is it
No more fun
The death of all joy
Has come.

Do you dare
Deny my

Potency
My kindness
Or forgiveness?
Just try
You will fry
Like the rest
In holiness

And not for a
Penny
Will I spare
Any time
For you
Ghost children
Down there
In the frightening world

You are alone
& have no need of other?
You and the child mother
Who bore you?
Who weaned you?
Who made you man?

In the true existence
I have risen above
Not of physical plains
Preached by the physicists
Who in discontent, claim
To know what they
Cannot in order
To save face

Hear me
Touch me
Sense the direction
Of yourself
Within &
Rise in spirit
To the established destiny
Open the doorway in heart, too
Let the only real presence in!

lll

Photo-booth killer
Fragile bandit
Straight from ambush

Kill me!
Kill the child who made
Thee.
Kill the thought provoking
Senator of lust
Who brought you to this state.

Kill hate
Disease
Warfare
Sadness

Kill badness
Kill madness

Kill photo mother murder tree
Kill me.
Kill yourself
Kill the little blind elf.

The beautiful monster
Vomits a stream of watches
Clocks jewels knives silver
Coins & copper blood

The well of time & trouble
Whiskey bottles perfume
Razor blades beads
Liquid insects hammers
& thin nails the feet of
birds eagle feathers & claws
machine parts chrome
teeth hair shards of
pottery & skulls the ruins
of our time the debris by
a lake the gleaming
beer cans & rust & sable
menstrual fur

Dance naked on broken
Bones feet bleed & stain
Glass cuts cover your mind
&  the dry end of vacuum

boat while the people
drop lines in still pools
and pull ancient trout
from the deep home.
Scales crusted & gleaming green
A knife was stolen. A
Valuable hunting knife

**By some strange boys
From the other camp across
The lake.**

Glisten shadows, call
Through the night.
The seekers seek
As the root sits content
Knowing to prepare for winter,
It retracts its growth as those in shallow
Splendor of coin & wealth expose themselves
Higher.

The boys will never find peace
Aloft to grace,
They bleed to an
Empty serpent.
The lake darkens in
Futile blood,
As the knife cuts through
Soulless flesh.

Permanent textured sighs
Virgin no more cries
Attracting only the flies
Feeding insects reap amongst the lies
Scavenger birds circle above a
Dieing existence in anticipation
Of what is to come.

The poison isles
The poison

Take this thin granule
Of evil snakeroot
From the southern
Shore

Way out miracle
Will find thee

The chopper blazed over
Inward click & sure
Blasted matter, made
The time bombs free
Of leprous
Lands
Spotted
W/ hunger
& clinging to law

Please
Show us your ragged head
& silted smiling eyes
calm in fire
a silky flowered shirt

edging the eyes, alive
spidery, distant
dial lies

come, calm one
into the life-try

already wife like
laten, leathery, loose
lawless, large & lanquid
she was a kingdom-cry
legion of lewd marching
mind-men

Where are your manners
Out there on the sunlit
Desert
Boundless
Galaxies of dust
Cactus spines, beads.
Bleach stones, bottles
& rust cars, stored for shaping

the new man, time-soldier
picked his way narrowly
thru the crowded ruins
of once grave city, gone
comic now w/ rats
& the insects of refuge

He lives in cars
Goes fruitless thru
The frozen schools
& finds no space
in shades of obedience

The monitors are silenced
The great graveled guard-towers
Sicken on westward beach
So tired of watching

If only one horse were left
To ride thru the waste
A dog at his side
To sniff meat-maids
Chained on the public poles

There is no more argument
in beds, at night
blackness is burned
stare into the parlors of town
where a woman dances
in her European gown
to the great waltzes
this could be fun
to rule a wasteland?

Debutante royalty sit
Atop the throne's of
Aged marble as it withers
in decay to the rot
Moss coated dampness
Reeks of the destruction

Skeletons left perched in
Midlothian splendor
Tarnished crowns
Mock their rule
Sparkless gems
Shine empty to
The order
Paradise made ruins


A choice brought forth by man

ll

Cherry palms
Terrible shores
& more
& many more

This we know
That all are free
In the school-made
Text of the unforgiving
Deceit smiles
Incredible hardships are suffered
By those barely able
To endure

But all will pass
Lie down in green grass
& smile, & muse, & gaze
up her smooth
resemblance
to the mating-Queen
who it seems
is in love
w/ the horseman

**Now, isn't that fragrant**
**Sir, isn't that knowing**
**W/ a wayward careless**
**Backward glance**
**The Hierarchy of the**
**Composed way is ageless**
**In attraction to the**
**Hand of the meek**

The rivers ascend to the sea
Lower then they
As humbleness controls
It's flow to greatness

Follow Spirit live in God
Low is high just exist
In pride of the self
Power in the word
Reward to the honor
Of virtues

# "A Goal of Universal Beings In Existence"

Greed can no longer rule in disguise as Lord, to the New Creatures.

Awareness is only the beginning. An action must follow for a reaction to take place once something is known for it to be.

Understand:

All can still be held accountable for past actions when they continue to act or exist in the same mindset of that past action, in an on going repetitive manner, generally, of poor intellect or character. No lesson has been learned. Growth has not been gained or achieved. Only time of itself has come to pass. A "Bee-line" for destruction continues. Existence has not progressed or moved forward but in reality, only continues to move parallel to a same existing plain not of the past but carried over into the given present. The past as yet, does not exist until the past is removed away from the present to an enlightened sense of positive growth experienced in a changed perception in action of all things which are then realized relative.

In change only, can all continue @ least here.

Awaken to the needed "Unity of All" for an earthly existence...

Please?

# About the Author

---

Forrest Parker is a simple man w/ a simple message. Raised in the Sandhill Ranch Country of North Central Nebraska, the only thing that needs to be said, is that unless the fronts can be united in Conservation, Peace & a World Changed Mentality, "The Shit" is just going to get pretty ugly

Lightning Source UK Ltd.
Milton Keynes UK
UKOW03f0250110517
300896UK00001B/204/P